Reaching Calm

REACHING CALM

Adhira Raju

*This book is dedicated to everyone
who's reaching their own calm.*

I hope this helps you get there.

Contents

ix   Foreword

2   Hello Fear

4   Who am I?

6   Block

8   Alone

10   Confusion

12   Lockdown

14   A Note to My Phone

16   Lifeline

18   Horizon

20   Finding Why

22   Reaching Calm

25   Acknowledgments

Foreword

Adhira's artistic inclinations were apparent from a very early age and they have only gotten stronger with the years. Her story about a blueberry gone bad was selected to be enacted as a play when she was in elementary school!

She is a voracious reader — books can't keep up with her — and a budding artist. Although she prefers reading prose, she jumped headfirst into the Youth Writer's Camp with characteristic dedication. We are very proud of the wonderful poems in this collection, her first work to be published. She is carrying on a tradition from her grandparents as an author!

We look forward to her growth as an artist, and as a person who cares deeply about the world around us.

Love,
Mom and Dad

REACHING CALM

Hello Fear

Hello, fear

I see you around a lot

You especially spend time
hanging around

New experiences
The future
What's happening in the world

Always hand in hand with
your friend, worry

You both are always guarding the good things
that come with taking risks

Thank you

When I make it past you,
that's victory

Who am I?

1. I am a lot of things,
   to the point where I get confused.

2. My name means moon.
   I'm someone who sometimes feel closer to
   the stars in space than
   hard reality.

3. I consider myself strange, but in a good way.

4. My zodiac signs are Virgo and the metal tiger. Hardworking, passionate, stubborn at times. That's definitely me.

5. Splashes of colorful ink.

6. Unfolding flowers.

7. Clear summer nights.

A strange list, but one that's truly me.

Block

Writer's block,
art block,

both just ways of describing
the feeling

when you stare down at

a notebook,
a sketchpad,
a canvas,
even a computer,

and see forbidding emptiness instead of possibility.

Block — even the word itself is something like a
brick wall, heavy and nearly impossible to move.

Why aren't my hands writing something?
Why can't I think of what I want to put here?

Should I just forget about it and do something else?

So many words, shapes, colors,
spinning and dancing
just out of reach.

Alone

Alone.

Alone means that
you don't have someone that will stay with you
for both your wins and your losses.

Alone means that
you don't have someone who you
can trust to listen to your fears.

Alone means that
you don't have someone who will take a stand with you.

Alone is being voiceless because
there's no one to hear you.

The opposite of alone is together.

Together is a community, a community of people
that you trust to hear you.

Together is when you can win as a group,
cheering for everyone else and yourself,

and together is when you can lose as a group,
laughing about it afterwards.
Together can even just be one person who'll listen,
because together is when you're not alone.

Confusion

Why do I wake up and decide how I feel by
looking at the sky?

So many little things confuse me,
making my emotions sway back and forth.

Wherever we are, I might suddenly
drop my voice and not want to talk,
or jump into the conversation,
excited and ready.

Constantly switching between sunny and cloudy.

If I'm nervous about something,
I'll think about it for days
before I actually have to do it.

How long will it take you to finish?

That simple question gives me so much trouble,
because I really don't know the answer.

Lockdown

Lockdown was...
strange.

A jumble of messy, yet distinct memories.

My third grade teacher telling us
that school would be out for a couple of weeks,
just as a safety measure.

Struggling to figure out online meetings for class.

Walking through our neighborhood in the evening,
watching the sky fade to painted pastel colors.

For those two-ish years, our entire world was a bubble
consisting of our house,
the greenery-covered streets we'd go for walks on,
and our glowing computer screens.

When lockdown began,
I was too little to realize what was happening.

I just remember feeling like a mouse in its hole,
warm and cozy,
not realizing everything Covid-19 was doing.

After the lockdown,
bit by bit,
the world started to open up.
Masks weren't mandatory.
Schools and offices were in person.

The bubble had slowly melted away,
and we were part of the world again.

A Note to My Phone

Hello, phone.

I have to write on you, even though
my typing is rather mediocre on phone,
decent at best.

Why?

Because paper is
far.
too.
distracting.

My writing space in my workbook, as of now, is
filled with doodles.

This is what my brain does when it's bored:
it runs in circles.

Scratch that — more like
strange, vexing, bending loops
around some void.

If my legs were half as good at running as my brain,
I could be in the Olympics.

My hands, though, are quite good at running.

When I'm jumpy, my hands automatically grab a pencil
and toss my nervousness all over whatever
scratch paper or math homework is available.

Usually, my brain is not bored with whatever situation
I'm in, but my hands, are, unfortunately,
not so easy to please:
they always need to be scratching down lines
while my mind focuses.

It's a strange way of focusing on something,
but it works.

Most of the time, anyways.

The real problem occurs when I'm
trying to accomplish something else
on that same paper — like writing.

In conclusion, dear phone,
that is why this note is being written to you now.

I hope you can understand.

Lifeline

When I'm standing on the shore
wading into

upset feelings
arguments
hard situations
things that scare me

I keep my lifelines with me

Music
Art
Stories

Instrumental notes swirling,
pencil scratching,
pages turning

Just for a little while,
taking me to a place where I don't have
worries or fears,
stopping the downpour

I'll always reach the shore with my lifelines

Horizon

I used to get upset so easily,
nervousness
taking over the wheels,
shoving me into the backseat

Thoughts in a storm,
tumbling through my head like
sleet and hail through the sky,
stopping me from thinking calmly
about anything.

I still do get upset.

I'm learning, though,
that just

taking a moment, to think and to breathe,
can help me choose where I'm going again

and let me see the horizon —
a horizon that's pink, orange, glowing,
a little stormy, but bright.

Finding Why

How do you find something?

Start with a question,
and another,
and another.

Now what?
Keep thinking.

What if I run from what I'm trying to find?

Can you find something if you run from it?

Think about all the little things.
Interests, emotions, facts, all coming together

Trying to answer that question: why?

Reaching Calm

Frustration
Worries
Anger

Choking

When you're upset,
you don't *want* to calm down,

and that's the problem.

Negative emotions kind of
pull you along
until you're completely convinced that

you're the only one who's right.

Still, underneath those rolling waves of what feels
more like tar than water,
there's a calm waiting,

the calm of an apology,
a compromise,
the end of an argument.

Time and taking the first step
are the only things that can
get you to that calm.

Acknowledgments

I would like to thank everyone who helped guide me through this crazy process!

First, to my mom, thank you so much for spending all that time looking over my poems and telling me what I needed. Secondly, thank you to my brother for being someone who I can always relate to and motivating me when I was writing this. Thank you to my dad for the constructive criticism and all the support on the poems I was really unsure about.

Thank you to everyone at the Youth Writer's Camp for making all this possible — Mr. Brandon for taking the time to teach us how to use our voices; Ms. Emily for the infinite help formatting and arranging; Shaniese for the dedicated emails recounting everything we needed; Ms. Stephanie for the amazing mental health sessions; all of our guest speakers; and, of course, my fellow youth writers for surrounding me with inspiration and fun!!!

About the Author

Adhira is an aspiring author and artist who loves to read, write, draw, and dream. This is her first time writing poetry and her first book, and she's looking forward to more of it!

youthwriterspress.com

A program of Youth Writer's Camp, Inc., Youth Writer's Press exists to create a safe space where young voices are heard, valued, and amplified. We are dedicated to producing and publishing work that allows youth to share their truths with the world. Our mission is to equip the next generation of writers with the resources, confidence, and platform to turn their stories into lasting works that resound far beyond the page.

youthwriterscamp.com

This book was created as part of Youth Writer's Camp, Inc., a nonprofit organization whose mission is to motivate communities to redefine hope for young people through mentoring, enrichment, and creativity.

In our workshops and programs, we blend literacy enrichment, social-emotional development, and creative entrepreneurship — using writing as a tool for healing, growth, and community connection.

Youth Writer's Camp Values:

COURAGE Creating the strength to face challenges with confidence.

RESILIENCE Creating the ability to bounce back and keep moving forward.

EMPATHY Creating connections by truly understanding others' feelings.

AUTHENTICITY Creating a space where you can be your true self without masks.

TRANSPARENCY Creating an atmosphere of openness and honesty, where vulnerability is valued.

ENTERPRISING Creating opportunities through innovation and a dynamic mindset.